Family Matters™

BEHIND THE SCENES

by T. R. Storey

Troll Associates

Steve with Urkelbot and Laurabot.

Published by Troll Associates, Inc.
STEVE URKEL, FAMILY MATTERS, characters, names, and all related indicia
are trademarks of Lorimar Television ©1993.

Printed in the United States of America.

10 9 8 7 6 5 4 3 2 1

Produced by Creative Media Applications, Inc.
Art direction by Fabia Wargin.

THIS BOOK IS DEDICATED TO MARCIE AND MICHAEL.

Special Thanks to Roy Wandelmaier, Sheryl Haft, Michelle Sucillon,
Amy Weingartner, and Carole Franklin.

TABLE OF CONTENTS

MEET THE CAST

The doorbell rings at the Winslow home.

"I'll get it!" shouts pretty Laura, who is dressed and ready for her surprise date. Laura dashes to the door and swings it open. Then she lets out a small shriek.

Standing before her is the strangest-looking individual she's ever seen. His pants ride up, way over his waist. They are held up by suspenders. The cuffs of these "flood pants" reveal at least five inches of sock. On his face sits a pair of glasses big enough to

INTRO- DUCTION

be the windshield of a 747.

"Good evening, my pet," says the young man, in a high squeaky voice. He flashes Laura a big smile and proceeds to kiss her hand. She doesn't know whether to laugh, cry, or call the police.

Who is this weird guy? Steve Urkel, of course! The coolest nerd to ever stroll across your TV screen.

Welcome to the world of *Family Matters*. In this new book, you'll read all about the Winslow family and their frequent house guest, supernerd Steve Urkel. You'll find out how *Family Matters* was born. You'll discover how the character of Steve Urkel was created, and how things changed when he joined the cast.

Take a look at the *Family Matters* checklist to see how many episodes you've seen and how many you've missed. Finally, we challenge you to take the Official *Family Matters* Trivia Quiz to see how much you know about the show and cast.

So dig in. Urkel, Laura, Eddie, and the whole *Family Matters* gang are ready and waiting for you!

Urkel and Eddie.

IN THE BEGINNING

1 **In 1989 producers Thomas L. Miller and Robert L. Boyett were proven talents.** They had already created a bunch of hit shows, like *Happy Days*, which starred Ron Howard, and *Mork and Mindy*, which launched the career of super-funnyman Robin Williams.

They also produced hit movies like *Silver Streak*, which starred Richard Pryor and Gene Wilder, and *Foul Play*, featuring Chevy Chase.

Then, Miller and Boyett did it again. They put their ever-creative minds together and came up with the idea for a new show. This one was about a Chicago policeman, his wife, and their three kids. That's how *Family Matters* was born!

JoMarie Payton plays Harriette on the show.

According to the producers, the overriding thought behind the show was, "If only their house was as big as their hearts!" This is the story of a warm, big-hearted family. There's lots of love, but not too much room!

Living quarters get even tighter when the wife's sister and her child move in. Space is stretched to the limit when the father's mother takes up residence as well. It's a good thing the members of this family really love each other!

When Miller and Boyett went to put *Family Matters* together, they started with JoMarie Payton. (She plays the part of Harriette on the show.) JoMarie had grown very popular with TV audiences as the elevator operator on the hit Miller-Boyett sitcom *Perfect Strangers*. They decided to feature her as the mother on their new comedy, *Family Matters*. The new show would come on right before *Perfect Strangers* on Friday nights.

"I really thought I was being fired from *Perfect Strangers*," JoMarie recalls when she was called into the producer's office. "When they told me I was getting a spinoff, I almost had a heart attack! I love the type of shows Tom and Bob create. I was thrilled to be involved with another one."

What exactly is a Tom Miller and Bob Boyett type of show?

They start with the idea of a family, but not just a family of characters. They like the cast and even the crew to feel like they are one big family, all working together.

The family idea also applies to their viewers. When Miller and Boyett created *Family Matters*, they set out to develop a show that both kids and parents would enjoy. *Family Matters* is a show *everyone* wants to watch!

Once JoMarie Payton was selected to star in the show, Miller and Boyett carefully auditioned hundreds of actors for the remaining roles. They came up with the talented cast you see each week, including Reginald VelJohnson (Carl), Telma Hopkins (Rachel), Kellie Shanygne Williams (Laura), Darius McCrary (Eddie), and Rosetta LeNoire (Mother Winslow).

This creative group pulled together to become an ensemble acting company. That means that instead of relying on one or two big stars, the actors all play off each other beautifully. The *Family Matters* cast members soon got to know each other and became more of a family. Viewers came to see the characters, more and more, as a *real-life* family. The show began to take off.

There was, however, one more element to be added to the mix before the *Family Matters* "family" would be complete. Little did the cast know, but the show was about to zoom to the upper stratosphere of success!

Full cast on set in 1940s costumes, from the episode called "Farewell My Laura."

2 **It was supposed to be only a one-shot deal.**
A one-time appearance. One of the show's
writers had come up with the funny idea of sending
Laura Winslow on the nightmare date of all time.
They had to create a character for her to go out with
who was such a total nerd that the audience would
feel sorry for Laura and laugh as soon as her date
walked on screen.

On March 23, 1990, Jaleel White walked on
screen as Steve Urkel for the first time. Audiences

ENTER URKEL

have been laughing
ever since.

"I created this
person in my
mind," says Jaleel
White. Jaleel
auditioned for the
role when he was 13 years old. He came up with
most of the ideas for the Urkel character himself.

"I went into the audition with the whiny voice,
thinking of not so much a nerd, as a lovesick
teenager. I knew that Urkel would fall for Laura the
minute he set eyes on her. Once I put on the
costume and the big glasses, hitched up the pants, did
the walk and the voice, it was like the character just
possessed me."

Rolling up the pants and wearing them way up

high were Jaleel's ideas. The ridiculously huge glasses ended up on Jaleel's face almost by accident.

"They're really my dad's glasses," Jaleel explains. "He's a dentist and he wears these oversized glasses to keep particles from flying into his eyes when he does dental work. On the way to the audition I was looking for the patented black-rimmed nerd glasses with a piece of tape in the middle. I couldn't find them and it was time to go. So my dad said, 'Just throw these on and come on, let's go.' "

The glasses turned out to be perfect for the character. Everyone at the audition loved them.

"I thought of getting different ones later," recalls Jaleel, "but

And he just keeps hanging around . . .

then I figured, if they work, don't mess with them!"

Jaleel wore them again for the callback auditions. (Actors usually go through a series of auditions before getting a part. The second, third, and so on auditions are known as "callbacks.")

Family Matters producer Tom Miller recalls the day Jaleel auditioned for the role of Urkel. "When he started the reading, the whole room screamed. I turned to my partner, Bob Boyett, and said, 'We have to use this kid!'"

At that moment Miller and Boyett decided Urkel was worth more than a one-shot appearance. They signed him up for occasional guest spots. At the taping of Urkel's hilarious first appearance, the character's "occasional" status was changed to "regular." As the show's ratings grew, so did Urkel's airtime. In fact, every *Family Matters*' script now must contain at least a little Urkel.

Why is Urkel so popular?

Think about the kids you go to school with. Some might be cool, others might not be. Urkel is definitely uncool, but he doesn't know it. He doesn't realize that others view him as a nerd. He thinks he's just one of the guys.

Urkel is always upbeat and positive. He's a real optimist. He's also brave, thoughtful, and kind.

If you met someone like that at school, it would

be pretty hard to dislike that person, no matter how much of a nerd he seems to be.

Jaleel White's portrayal of Urkel sent *Family Matters* soaring to the top of the ratings chart. It is now the number-one rated show in its time slot.

The addition of Urkel's character allowed the show to use more than one type of comedy. *Family Matters* always used the kind of comedy that comes out of everyday family situations. When the wacky character Urkel was added, the jokes and situations could also become outrageous.

The other cast members had worked together as one big happy family for most of the first season. It was only natural that they would feel a bit jealous when the focus of the show turned to Urkel. But in the end, they all realized Jaleel's character made the whole show better.

"At first my ego was bruised a little," admits Reginald VelJohnson (Carl Winslow). "But then I realized the outrageousness of the character blended in perfectly with our family." In fact the

Urkel, Laura, and Carl.   13

experienced Reginald and newcomer Jaleel soon became good friends.

Telma Hopkins (Rachel) agrees with her co-star. "It doesn't matter who on the show is shining at the moment. The longer the show stays on, the more we all have a chance to shine. Each of us gets to display our talents."

It's pretty obvious that Urkel is well loved by his fellow actors, the critics, and most of all by *Family Matters* fans everywhere.

In fact, the only person who may not love Steve Urkel is a certain TV

Carl and Laura.

scriptwriter. This writer is a friend of *Family Matters* co-executive producer Michael Warren. His name just happens to be . . . Steve Erkel.

Michael Warren named his TV nerd, *Urkel,* after his real-life friend, *Erkel.* Amazingly enough, Warren and Erkel are still friends!

3 **If someone had told extremely shy Kellie Shanygne Williams,** when she was a kid, that one day she would star in a hit TV show, she would have thought they were crazy.

Kellie Shanygne (pronounced "Sha-neen") Williams was born on March 22, 1976, in Washington, D.C., which is where she grew up. Her mother, Patricia, worked for *Jet* magazine. Her father, Ervin, was a manager at the telephone company. It

KELLIE SHANYGNE WILLIAMS

was Kellie's father who encouraged his daughter to begin acting.

But it wasn't future stardom Ervin Williams had on his mind when he brought his little girl to acting classes.

"In the beginning," Kellie recalls, "my father put me into the acting classes when I was four because I was an introvert. I was really shy. I wouldn't talk to anybody. Then in the classes I started singing, dancing, and acting. I guess I came out of my shell."

Did she ever! By age six, pretty Kellie was working as a runway model, modeling children's clothing. It was also around that time that Kellie picked up her nicknames.

Her mother called her "Monkey."

Kellie explains. "My aunt owns two cleaners, and I used to go there after school and swing on the bars in the cleaners."

Her other nickname is "Beanie."

"I had a 'bean' head," says Kellie, "and I didn't grow hair until I was five years old."

Her acting career began at the age of six, with a stage role in a play called *Cousins*.

The following year Kellie signed with an agent. She continued to appear in live theater productions and began to get cast in TV commercials.

From there her career took off. She appeared at the prestigious Kennedy Center for the Performing Arts in Washington. The shows included *Goin' Home* and *Birthday Celebration*—a tribute to Dr. Martin Luther King, Jr. She also appeared in stage productions at the International Drama Festival in Dundalk, Ireland, and Nassau, Bahamas.

Her recent pre-*Family Matters* work includes the 1986 television tribute to Dr. Martin Luther King, Jr. called *Celebration Fit for a King*, and the feature films *Men Don't Leave* and *Suspect*. During all this time, Kellie continued to attend school as she always had.

Then in late 1989, Kellie's agent told her about a new TV series that was casting in New York and Los Angeles. Kellie sent in a videotape of her work, and

Steve and Laura at Rachel's Place in "Farewell My Laura."

was asked to come out to Los Angeles for an audition. The rest, of course, is *Family Matters* history!

Kellie and her mom moved out to Los Angeles, where *Family Matters* is taped. Although Kellie is thrilled with her role on the series, she sometimes regrets leaving school and all her friends in Washington.

"I have a tutor, so I go to school at the studio," Kellie explains, "but I miss my old friends. It's boring sometimes, staying in a room alone all day to study."

Then again, she's not exactly alone. She's got her good friend, Jaleel White, to keep her company while studying—when they're not busy being Laura and Urkel, that is!

How did Kellie feel when Urkel joined the show?

At first she got tired of people always saying the same thing to her. "Tell us about Urkel," they would say. "Is he really a nerd?"

"Don't you want to know about *me*?" she asks with a smile. "But I guess if I were them, I'd want to know about him, too."

Kellie was not pleased originally about being known as Urkel's girlfriend or about the shift in focus on the show to Urkel's character.

"I think we pretty much knew it was going to happen," Kellie explains. "You could see how much the audience loved his character, and how funny he was, so his popularity wasn't a surprise."

But Kellie also loves what the character has done for the show. She has become great friends with Urkel's alter ego, actor Jaleel White. "We have fun together. We eat lunch together every day. He's just like my brother or something."

What about Laura and Urkel's romance? Will they ever get together?

"I do think Laura loves him," says Kellie. "I think in time she'll realize that he really loves her, and he would be a good person to take care of her. Then she'll snatch him right up!"

It sounds like Kellie knows Laura pretty well. And that's not surprising, since she feels her character is not that different from herself in real life.

"We're very similar," she tells. "She's just like me. We say the same things, and we both just say what we feel. We're both strong-willed. We know what we want. The only way we differ is in our taste in clothes. Laura dresses much more conservatively than I do!"

Kellie has also become good friends with Telma Hopkins (Rachel). "I go over to her house almost every weekend," says Kellie. "She's like my second mom. She's also helped me with my acting. She tells me to commit to what I'm doing when I work on my character and my dialogue."

When she's not busy acting or studying, Kellie's favorite thing to do is go shopping in the great stores of L.A. "I buy clothes that are funky with lots of colors," she says.

This active teen loves roller skating, swimming, and bicycle riding. She's also excellent at the street sport of double-dutch rope jumping.

Kellie is not allowed to start dating until she's 16. But when she does, she knows exactly the kind of boy she'd like to go out with.

"Anybody who remotely resembles my father in any kind of way!" she explains. "Someone with his sense of humor—he tells those corny jokes, those father jokes. Just a nice guy, someone who's laid back. Someone like my father."

The walls of Kellie's room at home are covered with posters of her favorite celebrities like Janet Jackson and Yosemite Sam. She also collects stuffed animals.

Kellie lives in Los Angeles when *Family Matters* is taping. When she's not working on the show, Kellie returns to the Maryland suburb where the Williamses now make their home. She lives with her folks, her 11-year-old sister, Marti, and her 10-year-old brother, Donte.

As for Kellie's future, she hasn't made up her mind. "I think I want to be a director. But sometimes I think I'd like to be a lawyer. I'm still debating." Whatever talented Kellie Shangyne Williams decides about her future, you can bet it will be a be a bright one!

4 As Eddie Winslow on *Family Matters,*

Darius McCrary gives viewers a look at the problems of a bright teenager who's always looking for an angle. Eddie's constantly trying to get away with some scheme. It could be faking all A's on his report card, shooting pool for money, or driving before he has his license. For Darius McCrary, *his* success has come from hard work, talent, and a little bit of luck.

Darius was born on May 1, 1977, in Los Angeles, California. His parents knew they had a talented child on their hands very early on. At the age

of two, young Darius performed a duet at a concert with his father. His father just happens to be a famous gospel singer and composer named Howard McCrary.

At the age of ten, Darius' aunt, Chip Fields, an actress and director, suggested he try out for a role in a feature film called *Big Shots.*

"The whole audition thing was new to me," recalls Darius. "It was weird. I mean, here I was with all these kids, and I didn't think I was going to get the part. All of them were professional. After the

Scene from episode called "Old and Alone."

audition I flew to Detroit with my aunt. It was there I got the call."

Darius got called back to Los Angeles for a taping. Then he was flown out to Chicago with four other boys, where the final decision was made. Darius McCrary got the part and his first acting role.

"Needless to say, it was the biggest break of my life," he says.

His appearance in *Big Shots* led to more work for Darius. He made his first television appearances in 1987 with guest shots on *Hooperman* and *Amen*. Darius also appeared in the Oscar-winning film *Mississippi Burning*, where he earned excellent reviews for his work with Gene Hackman.

"I played a character named Aaron Williams," he explains. "He was sort of like a young Martin Luther King. He stood up and did what he felt was right."

After these appearances, Darius decided acting was what he wanted to do with his life.

And then came *Family Matters*.

"When I went in to audition for *Family Matters*, I just hit it right off with the producers," tells Darius. "There was another boy up for the part of Eddie. I half jokingly said to the producers, 'Pick me!' And they did! They told me they wanted to go with the look I had because they were trying to create a heartthrob type of image."

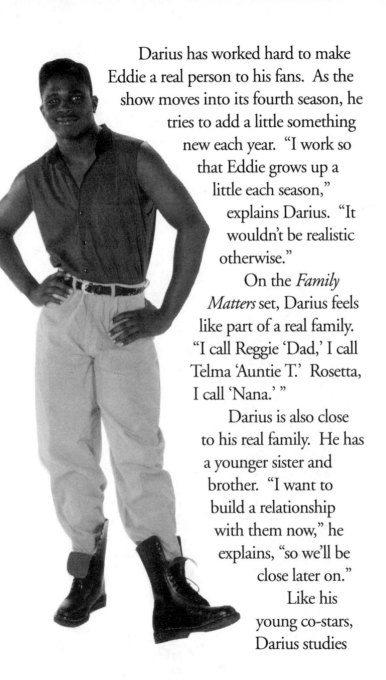

Darius has worked hard to make Eddie a real person to his fans. As the show moves into its fourth season, he tries to add a little something new each year. "I work so that Eddie grows up a little each season," explains Darius. "It wouldn't be realistic otherwise."

On the *Family Matters* set, Darius feels like part of a real family. "I call Reggie 'Dad,' I call Telma 'Auntie T.' Rosetta, I call 'Nana.'"

Darius is also close to his real family. He has a younger sister and brother. "I want to build a relationship with them now," he explains, "so we'll be close later on."

Like his young co-stars, Darius studies

with a tutor on the set. "I like having a tutor because I don't have to worry about being distracted in class and getting in trouble. The other kids on the show are really cool, so I like being around them."

When Darius is not working on school or *Family Matters*, sports and music fill his time. He's an excellent athlete who enjoys football, swimming, golf, basketball, soccer, and karate.

Eddie, Urkel, and Waldo.

On the musical side, he plays drums and keyboards, and sings. In fact he has already recorded an album. "It's pop tunes," says Darius. "Marvin Gaye, James Brown, Bobby Brown, that kind of stuff. Some upbeat, some ballads."

As far as girlfriends go, Darius is too busy for one right now. And one is all he really ever wants. "I want to date just one girl," he reveals, "not a lot at one time, because the pattern you set now is the pattern you set for life. When I get married, I'm only going to have one wife!"

He does, however, love being recognized by lots of girls he meets. "It's cool being recognized on the street," admits Darius. "I like being good to my fans and signing autographs. You never know what someone else is going through. They could be having a terrible day. When you're a celebrity, you owe so much to your fans."

What does the future hold for this multitalented actor, singer, dancer, and musician? "I definitely plan to continue acting and recording albums," explains Darius. "But I'm also planning on going to the UCLA Medical Center to study to become a heart surgeon. That's one thing I'm aiming for."

Who knows? Maybe someday we'll be watching a show starring *Doctor* Eddie Winslow, or should we say, Dr. Darius McCrary, heartthrob/heart surgeon!

5 **Practically overnight, the character of Steve Urkel** transformed *Family Matters* into the hottest show on television. Jaleel White's rise to success as an actor, however, has taken a number of years.

"I've been in showbiz for 13 years," explains Jaleel.

For an actor to work that long before achieving big success is not unusual. What is unusual in Jaleel's case is that he's only 16 years old!

Jaleel White was born on November 27, 1976, in a suburb of Los Angeles. He is the only child of

JALEEL WHITE

Michael White, a dentist, and Gail White.

When he was three years old, Jaleel's preschool teacher, Mrs. Lew, saw what she called "a spark of comedic talent" in the toddler. She saw he was unusually witty and charming, and he easily made her and the rest of his preschool class laugh.

Mrs. Lew suggested to Jaleel's parents that they try to get the boy into show business. Gail White registered her son in an acting workshop, where he was discovered by a top children's casting agent, Iris Burton.

Young Jaleel started to get work in TV commercials immediately. He made his acting debut in a Goodyear tire ad. "My part in the commercial was to swing on a tire and go 'Wheee!' " recalls Jaleel.

By the time he was nine, he had appeared in more than 30 TV commercials for such products as Kellogg's breakfast cereals, Atari computers, Nabisco cookies, Pepsi, Toys 'R' Us, and McDonald's. His favorite commercial was the one he did for Jell-O Pudding Pops with the one and only Bill Cosby!

Being a star in TV commercials never went to Jaleel's head. "When you start as young as I did, you don't really know what you're doing. By the time you are seven or eight you realize, hey, you're on TV, but by then you're so comfortable with it, it's no big deal."

Jaleel soon moved from commercials to roles on television shows. He had a regular role on *Charlie & Company*, and made guest appearances on *The Jeffersons* and *Mr. Belvedere*.

He began to get work in TV movies like *Kids Don't Tell*, *The Leftovers*, *Silence of the Heart*, and *Camp Cucamonga*. He also appeared in the *Jay Leno Family Special*, a variety show.

Jaleel White was happy. His acting work fit into the life of a normal teen. Most of his time was spent on school, sports, and his friends. He also has a number of hobbies that kept him busy. They include writing, drawing cartoons, cooking, and making homemade ice cream.

Then came Urkel, *Family Matters*, and superstar popularity. Has all this success changed Jaleel White? "I haven't changed at all," he insists. "It's the people around me who've changed."

Jaleel sometimes has a hard time with old friends who feel like they have to treat him differently now.

This quiet, thoughtful young man never boasts about his achievements or his position in the *Family Matters* cast. He is very considerate of the other actors' feelings, and is, in fact, his own toughest critic.

"I critique my own performance," says Jaleel. "And I'm not always satisfied with my work. I see myself doing things the general public wouldn't see, and I go back and correct them in the next show. I'm

Assistant propman talking to Jaleel.

definitely looking for the little bitty fine points I have to make sure are up to par."

Off-screen, Jaleel dresses casually, mostly in basketball shorts, shirts, shoes, and caps. That might clue you in to one of Jaleel's major passions— basketball. He loves to watch "his (L.A.) Lakers" play. He even got to sit courtside for a Lakers game and meet the team afterward.

Jaleel is also a pretty good player. "Shooting hoops is my way of letting off steam," says Jaleel. He shone in a recent celebrity basketball game to raise money for charity, outplaying *Beverly Hills 90210* star Luke Perry, and rapper Marky Mark. At that charity game Jaleel got to meet and play with his two basketball heroes, Magic Johnson and Michael Jordan. He also collects basketball cards.

Despite his acting success, Jaleel still faces a home life filled with regular chores and rules. He feels his upbringing has kept him on the right track in life. It's hard to become a spoiled superstar when you still have to clean your own room!

The Whites have always been loving parents. They are strict, but fair. Jaleel still has to pitch in and do his share around the house. Just because he's famous doesn't mean he gets out of doing his chores.

More than anything, Jaleel's folks stress the importance of education. Even with all his success these days, Jaleel is still a straight-A student.

Just like Kellie Williams' folks, Jaleel's parents also have strict rules about dating. "My parents always said, 'No dating until I'm 16.' And knowing them, maybe even not at that time."

Still, Jaleel doesn't seem to be in a rush to begin dating. "Once you start dating, things can go absolutely nuts. Sometimes I think it's better to keep your sanity and stay away from dating for a while. That way you can at least get some good grades in school."

Still, Jaleel has lots of friends, including many girls. Kellie Shanygne Williams—Urkel's beloved Laura Winslow on *Family Matters*—is one of his best friends.

Most days find Jaleel at the Lorimar Studios taping *Family Matters*. His day starts in the makeup

Laura with "Romeo" in his suit of armor.

and wardrobe department, where his Urkel clothes and glasses go on. "I roll up my pants, put on suspenders, and you get the impression that the pants are too small. Actually, they're quite comfortable."

Over the course of the day, Jaleel is either shooting *Family Matters*, doing schoolwork with a tutor, reading his fan mail, eating lunch with his pal Kellie Williams, or visiting other buddies around the huge Lorimar lot.

"I know a zillion people here," says Jaleel. His friends include cast members from shows like *Perfect Strangers* and *Full House*.

Jaleel White realizes he is a role model to kids who watch *Family Matters*, and he takes that responsibility seriously. He's always telling kids he speaks with that above all else, school comes first. "The most important thing is to get your education. Without that, you don't have much."

As far as the future goes, Jaleel would like to eventually become a director. He's learning as much as he can about the craft right now on the set of *Family Matters*. He's always asking about lighting, camera angles, and other important factors in becoming a good director.

For now, though, he's happy to continue his work making us all laugh as Steve Urkel. "No sweat, my pet!"

Rachel Crawford's stay in her sister Harriette Winslow's home was supposed to be temporary. She turned to the emotional support of the Winslow family following the death of her husband. But after three seasons on the air, it's hard to picture the Winslow household without the warm, funny, and energetic presence of Rachel.

The reason for this, of course, is the multitalented singer/actress Telma Hopkins. She brings high energy and a strong positive life force to the character each week on *Family Matters*.

TELMA HOPKINS

"The show works so well because we (the cast) really believe in each other," explains Telma. "We've become close and care for each other. Each of us gets to display our talents." Telma certainly has many different talents to display.

She began her performing career as a backup singer for such superstars as Stevie Wonder, Marvin Gaye, Wilson

Pickett, Issac Hayes, Dionne Warwick, and the Four Tops.

"If you lived in Detroit," says Telma, "and you didn't work for GM, Ford, or Chrysler, you worked for Motown." Motown is the name of a famous music company that produced such stars as the Jackson Five, Diana Ross and the Supremes, and the Temptations.

She went on to greater success in the 1970s as a member of the singing group Tony Orlando and Dawn. The group had a series of hit records and starred in a TV variety show that ran for four years.

Telma made her television acting debut as Daisy in the ground-breaking mini-series *Roots: The Next Generation*. From there she went on to star in *Bosom Buddies* with Tom Hanks, *The New Odd Couple*, and *Gimme A Break*. She also appeared in the feature films *Vital Signs*, *Trancers*, and *Pulse Pounders*.

Telma Hopkins has been successful in both the music and acting fields. Which does she prefer?

"I've found that acting suits me better the older I get," she reveals. "The lifestyle is more normal than being on the road (a common situation for musicians). I like going home every day. I need that stability."

Telma believes the character of Rachel is closer to her own personality than any other role she's ever played. "She's a single parent like me"—Telma has a

Rachel singing at Rachel's Place.

20-year-old son in college—"she's very earthy, very worldly. I love kids, and Rachel has a lot of kid in her, and more than a little bit of comedienne."

Telma's comedic inspirations growing up were Carol Burnett, whom she idolized, and Pearl Bailey, whom she calls "A lady of great attitude."

Telma is quick to say what a great experience *Family Matters* continues to be for her. "All of us in *Family Matters* really work hard to make it a family show that really is about a family. There's something for everyone because we have three generations under one roof. And we stick together."

Off the set, Telma enjoys cooking, reading, and collecting antiques. When asked what she'd like to do in the future, Telma replies, "I want to do everything under the rainbow, from singing and acting, to comedy and drama."

When Telma was growing up, her grandmother used to tell her she'd better get serious about her life because she'd never make a living being silly. Fortunately for *Family Matters'* fans, Grandma was wrong!

Rachel and Hariette in the episode called "The Good, the Bad, and the Urkel."

7 **When an actor's career is going well, one role leads to another.** That's exactly how Reginald VelJohnson came to star on *Family Matters.*

Many people first got to know (and like) him as police sergeant Al Powell, Bruce Willis' telephone buddy in the two *Die Hard* films.

"I never even thought I'd get the *Die Hard* part," recalls Reginald. "At the auditions, I heard the other actors yelling and screaming in the role. I thought I'd go soft. I thought it might work."

MEET THE CAST

REGINALD VELJOHNSON

Obviously it did! Reginald was well liked by everyone who saw *Die Hard,* including *Family Matters* co-creators Miller and Boyett. "They told me they really liked my character in *Die Hard*," recalls Reginald. "They thought I was someone the character of Harriette could play off of."

Reginald had already made one appearance on *Perfect Strangers* by the time Miller and Boyett decided to spin Harriette off into her own show. "They were just looking for the right chemistry for the husband on *Family Matters*," says Reggie, as his friends call him. With Reginald VelJohnson they found it!

Reginald grew up in New York City. From the time he was a child, no career other than acting ever entered his mind.

"At age six I made puppets out of socks and put on shows," he recalls. "I was in my first play in second grade." He continued to act in school productions throughout junior high and high school.

Reggie was graduated from New York University with a degree in theater. He began acting professionally in plays while he was still in college.

His first film was *Crocodile Dundee*, in which he played a chauffeur. He has also appeared in *Cotton Club*, *Ghostbusters*, and *Turner and Hooch*.

These days, Reggie couldn't be happier doing a weekly TV show. "I always liked the idea of doing a series," he explains. "To work on a character every week is a blast. We touch on certain things that speak directly to the viewers. It's nice that people are responding to what we're doing."

Because *Family Matters* didn't have a huge audience during its first season, Reggie expected the show to be canceled. "At first, people ignored us. I saved my money because I didn't think it would last. I thought we were good, but others didn't seem too excited. Our small following of loyal fans spread the word."

He credits the eventual success of the show to the genuine family feeling the characters have for each other. "We hang out with each other off the set. Also, we don't just play everything for laughs. Our show is mostly funny, but sometimes it has a little tinge of reality, a little dramatic moment to make it real, because after all, that's what you get in life."

You might be surprised to learn that off-camera, it's Reginald who's the biggest clown among the actors on the show. "Reggie keeps everyone loose," says co-star Kellie Shanygne Williams. "He's the practical joker of the cast."

As long as this teddy bear of a man with the big smile and warm heart continues to make people laugh (on- and off-screen), *Family Matters* should be around for a long time to come.

8 **It all started with JoMarie Payton.** Co-creators Tom Miller and Bob Boyett felt that her character of Harriette Winslow, the elevator operator on their hit show *Perfect Strangers*, was strong enough to support her own show. That show, of course, became *Family Matters*.

"The key to *Family Matters'* original success was Harriette," says JoMarie. "She grounds the show. She's different from any other mother on TV. She's everybody's favorite mom, favorite aunt, and the keeper of the neighborhood. She's someone

everybody knows, not someone everybody knows *about.*"

JoMarie feels the same way about the other characters on the show, as well. "I think the audience recognizes all the members of Harriette's family. They're all the sort of people you wouldn't be afraid to ask for directions or change for a dollar. They're people you can touch, people you can really communicate with."

JoMarie Payton was born in Albany, Georgia, and went to high school and college in Miami, Florida. She began acting and singing in high school

Myrtle, Harriette, and Rachel during a beauty treatment.

and knew that performing was what she really wanted to do. Her family supported her decision.

"My mother always trusted me to do the right thing," JoMarie recalls. "I used to write songs and perform in plays. She went to every performance I ever did from age six until I left home at 25."

JoMarie stayed in the Miami area after college. She now considers it her home. "I come back to Miami whenever I need to get juiced up," she explains. "Hollywood is a fantasy place. I come back to Miami for some reality."

JoMarie's big break came when she joined the touring company for the musical *Purlie*. The show ended its tour in Los Angeles, so JoMarie decided to stay out west and try to break into television. She was very successful. JoMarie appeared on such shows as *The Redd Foxx Variety Show, Frank's Place,* and *The Slap Maxwell Story.* Then she landed her role on *Perfect Strangers* and her career really took off.

Carl and Harriette.

JoMarie has also been in several movies including *Camp Beverly Hills,* *The Disorderlies,* and *Crossroads.*

Off the set, JoMarie devotes much of her time to volunteer work. She was honorary chairperson of Voting is a Family Matter, a local drive to register voters. She also donates her time to helping unwed mothers and the homeless.

There is even a volleyball tournament held every year, in her name, which raises money for scholarships for preschool and elementary schoolchildren.

The National Commission of Working Women honored JoMarie in 1990 for her outstanding portrayal of a working woman on *Family Matters.* For her commitment to the community, the city of Los Angeles and Mayor Tom Bradley honored JoMarie as Woman of the Year in 1991.

When she's not busy acting or helping others, she enjoys swimming, sewing, and music. She has one daughter who is eight years old, from her first marriage. Wedding bells will ring again for JoMarie, who is planning to get married in April 1993.

Her involvement with the community also extends to the community of *Family Matters* viewers. "I have suggested," she said, "that if there is anything portrayed in this show people are not satisfied with, that they don't think we do honestly, then they should please write in and let us know."

"I think we owe our audience the responsibility to be honest with them. That's my main concern. If we can be honest about a situation, be it gcod, bad, happy, sad, or whatever, then the show works for everybody."

JoMarie believes that *Family Matters* strikes a perfect balance. "We're not so rich that you're intimidated by us, and we're not so poor that you're afraid of us. We're just right there where you can reach us, and that's how I'd like for it to stay."

With JoMarie Payton as the mom of the Winslow household, you can be sure that *Family Matters* will stay right there—at the top of the TV comedy world.

9 **Carl may think he's the head of the Winslow household.** But everyone else, including *Family Matters'* loyal viewers, knows the real chief of this clan is Carl's mom, Mother Winslow. She is played to perfection by show-business veteran Rosetta LeNoire, who fills her character with strength, stubbornness, warmth, and humor.

In the very first episode of *Family Matters,* Carl's mother moves into the already-crowded Winslow home. It was Harriette who invited her to live with

ROSETTA LENOIRE

them. Carl didn't think much of the idea.

"Why not?" asked Harriette. "She seems like a nice lady."

"That's the holiday mother," said Carl. "The real mother is different. She takes over everything!"

Carl, of course, could not be more correct. Mother Winslow did succeed in taking over everything, making for some of *Family Matters'* funniest moments.

With her work on *Family Matters,* Rosetta LeNoire continues a show-business career that spans more than half a century. She recently celebrated her 80th birthday and her 67th year in show business!

Christmas Day at the Winslow house.

Rosetta LeNoire's childhood was not an easy one. Her mother died in childbirth, and baby Rosetta was born with a bone disease called rickets. As a young child she had to wear leg braces.

Rosetta went to a special school for the handicapped until she was 13. By then she was strong enough to walk without leg braces, and attend public school.

As a 13-year-old in the 1920s, she took music lessons from the famous piano player Eubie Blake. He was one of the inspirations of her life, and she still remembers the lessons he taught her.

"Eubie Blake taught me how to look up and be proud of myself," says Rosetta. "He said, 'A flower doesn't bloom unless it faces the sun.'"

At the age of 15 Rosetta became a chorus girl. She performed with her godfather Bill "Bojangles" Robinson, the legendary singer and dancer. She made her Broadway debut in 1939 in a show called *The Hot Mikado*. Rosetta has appeared in many Broadway and Off-Broadway plays since that time.

Rosetta made her television debut in the 1940s, during the very first years TV existed! Her first role was on a show called *Search for Tomorrow*.

More recently she has been on comedies like *Gimme A Break*, and the soap operas *Guiding Light* and *Another World*.

Rosetta has also appeared in many feature films, including *Moscow on the Hudson, The Sunshine Boys,* and *Brewster's Millions.*

In 1968 she decided to give something back to the profession that had given her so much. Rosetta founded the Amas (Latin for "you love") Musical Theater in New York City. In 1976 Rosetta decided she wanted to honor her teacher Eubie Blake. She founded the Eubie Blake Children's Theater in New York. The theater provides children, aged 9 to 16, with weekly classes in acting, singing, and dancing. Through the children's theater, Rosetta is able to pass Eubie Blake's positive outlook on to many children.

Rosetta LeNoire can now be seen providing warm, touching, and funny moments to television viewers. *Family Matters* wouldn't be complete without Mother Winslow!

Cast on the set of "The Good, the Bad, and the Urkel."

10 **Have you ever wondered how an episode of *Family Matters* is put together?** Here's a behind-the-scenes look at the fascinating process, from story idea to completed episode.

First the writers meet and discuss story ideas. They then choose the best ideas to make into episodes. A beat sheet is written next. A beat sheet describes each scene in the story in only a few sentences. A writer is assigned to write a ten-page outline, which describes the story in greater detail.

After the outline, the writer does a first version or first draft of the script. This includes what the characters will say, and what they are doing while they're saying their lines.

The *Family Matters'* staff does a rewrite on the script, changing it to make improvements. They make the jokes funnier. They also make sure the characters say and do things you'll recognize as something Eddie or Urkel would say or do.

The writer takes these changes and writes a final draft. This is the version of the script that will be given to the cast and crew.

Winslows in a flour fight.

A production meeting is held, in which the heads of the various departments meet to discuss what will be needed for the episode. The property or "prop" department figures out what props will be needed. A prop is an item used on the set, like a coffee cup or a pen.

The wardrobe department figures out what the actors will wear in the episode. The technical departments like special effects, lighting, and sound also attend the production meeting. So does the director of photography—who figures out how the episode will be taped. Dialogue coaches also.attend.

They see if the actors will need any help with accents or special voices.

Finally, the cast gets to see the script for the first time. They sit around a big table with the writers and read the script aloud, making further changes.

The cast rehearses for four days, working with the director on the set. When they're ready, the cast performs a run through, which is a performance of the entire script. The run through is watched by the writers and producers, who make any needed last-minute changes. For the final rehearsal, the cast rehearses in front of the cameras. This is so the cameramen can verify where they'll tape the actors and the director can give last-minute instructions.

Rehearsal time also happens to be practical-joke time on the set of *Family Matters*. The entire cast remembers the time Jaleel White, as Urkel, was tied to a bedpost for a scene in an upcoming show.

The director yelled "Cut!" and someone said, "Let's break for lunch. Bye, Jaleel!" Everyone on the set broke up laughing. On the show, Urkel is often stuck or locked up somewhere in an uncomfortable position. Leaving Jaleel in those binds has become a running joke among the cast and crew of the show!

Following the rehearsal period, it's show time!

The episode is filmed in front of a live audience, so the laughter you hear each week is real. The scenes are always taped in the same order you see them unless there is a shooting off the set. When a scene takes place off the set, it is called on location. After shooting all the scenes, the editor has ten days to do the first cut. A cut is a version of the show after the editor has put the scenes into the right order, and cut them to the right length. The length of each scene is important, because each episode, plus commercials, must fit exactly into one half hour. The time of the show is actually only between 22 and 23 minutes.

The producers view the first cut, make changes, and then the show is given back to the editor for the final cut. Music is written, recorded, and added. Sound effects—like footsteps, car engines, or phone rings—are put in. The credits—that's the information about the cast and crew that rolls up your screen when the show is finished each week— are added.

The show is now complete.

This entire process, from story idea to completed episode, takes only about six weeks.

Judy Winslow (Jaimee Foxworth).

11 How many of these *Family Matters* episodes have you seen?

FIRST SEASON, 1989–90

☐ 1) "The Mama Who Came to Dinner" — Carl's mother, Mother Winslow, moves in with the family.

☐ 2) "Short Story" — Rachel writes a short story based on the Winslow family, which gets everyone upset.

☐ 3) "Two-Income Family" — Harriette is fired from her job as an elevator operator at the *Chronicle*, then is rehired—as a security guard.

Your *Family Matters* CHECKLIST

☐ 4) "Basketball Blues" — Carl tries to train Eddie to be a basketball player, but Eddie has no interest in the sport.

☐ 5) "Rachel's First Date" — Rachel is a nervous wreck as she prepares to go on her first date since becoming a widow.

☐ 6) "Body Damage" — Rachel and Harriette wreck the classic police car Carl is supposed to drive in the Columbus Day Parade.

☐ 7) "Mr. Badwrench" — Carl attempts to put a shower in Mother Winslow's bathroom, with disastrous results.

☐ 8) "Straight A's" — Eddie comes home with straight A's on his report card, but Carl soon discovers that the card was faked on a friend's computer.

☐ 9) "False Arrest" — Carl arrests an actor known as "America's Favorite Dad," who tries to bribe his way out of the arrest.

☐ 10) "The Quilt" — Laura sells a quilt at a family garage sale. The quilt turns out to be a 200-year-old family heirloom.

☐ 11) "Stakeout" — Carl goes on a stakeout with his new partner—a gorgeous female police officer.

☐ 12) "The Big Reunion" — Carl is worried about going to his high school reunion because of his weight.

☐ 13) "Laura's Date" — Laura ends up with three dates to a party. This show marks Urkel's first appearance on *Family Matters*.

☐ 14) "Man's Best Friend" — The kids bring home a dog Carl doesn't like—until it starts chasing Urkel from the house.

☐ 15) "Baker's Dozen" — Rachel decides to market Carl's secret recipe for lemon-cream tarts.

Richie (Bryton McClure). 55

☐ 16) "The Candidate" — Eddie runs for president of the freshman class with Laura as his campaign manager.

☐ 17) "The Party" — Eddie is left to watch Judy and Laura while the adults go to a family birthday party. A wild party in the Winslow home results.

☐ 18) "The Big Fix" — Urkel helps Eddie with his algebra in exchange for a date with Laura.

☐ 19) "Sitting Pretty" — Rachel tries to tell the new man in her life she has a child, Eddie goes through a dating slump, Carl tries to impress his new captain, and Laura goes into the baby-sitting business.

☐ 20) "In a Jam" — Urkel pays Eddie to be his bodyguard and protect him from a school bully.

☐ 21) "Rock Video" — Eddie and his band, The Dreamers, make a rock video. Carl struggles with his income-tax return.

☐ 22) "Bowl Me Over" — Eddie is embarrassed when Laura beats him at a video game. Carl gets upset when Harriette beats him at bowling.

SECOND SEASON, 1990–91

☐ 1) "Rachel's Place" — Rachel opens a new, hip restaurant that becomes a local teen hangout—Rachel's Place.

☐ 2) "Marriage 101" — Laura gets matched up with Urkel in a mock marriage class at school.

☐ 3) "Boxcar Blues" — Carl and Urkel end up chasing a robber while teamed together on police patrol.

Scene from "Flashpants."

☐ 4) "Torn Between Two Lovers" — Urkel mistakenly thinks Rachel has fallen in love with him.

☐ 5) "Flashpants" — Carl and Harriette compete in the annual police officers' dance contest.

☐ 6) "Crash Course" — Eddie fails his driving test, but takes his new girlfriend out for a drive anyway.

☐ 7) "Cousin Urkel" — Steve Urkel's cousin, Myrtle Urkel, comes to town and falls for Eddie.

☐ 8) "Dedicated to the One I Love" — Laura sets Urkel up with a nerdy girl named Suzie.

☐ 9) "Fast Eddie Winslow" — Eddie, Urkel, and Rodney get involved with a pool hustler.

☐ 10) "Dog Day Halloween" — Dressed in Halloween costumes, Laura and Urkel are caught in an armed bank robbery.

☐ 11) "The Science Project" — Laura and Urkel team up for a school science project.

☐ 12) "Requiem for an Urkel" — Urkel gets into a boxing match with the school bully over taking Laura to the Sadie Hawkins dance.

☐ 13) "Son" — A family argument breaks out when Eddie loses Carl's screwdriver.

☐ 14) "Ice Station Winslow" — Carl takes Eddie on an ice-fishing trip.

☐ 15) "Have Yourself a Very Winslow Christmas" — Urkel spends Christmas with the Winslows.

☐ 16) "Do the Right Thing" — Carl finds a diamond bracelet and struggles over whether to keep it or not.

☐ 17) "High Hopes" — Carl deals with his fear of heights during a hot-air balloon ride with Urkel.

☐ 18) "Life of the Party" — Willie and Waldo crash a rooftop party thrown by Laura and Maxine.

☐ 19) "Fight the Good Fight" — Laura starts a petition to include a year-round class in black history at her school.

☐ 20) "Busted" — Urkel and Eddie go to an illegal gambling casino to try to win money to fix a dent that Eddie put in the family car.

☐ 21) "Finding the Words" — Harriette and Rachel's father, who abandoned them as kids, shows up at the Winslow house.

☐ 22) "Taking Credit" — Two stories about falsely taking the credit for something someone else did.

☐ 23) "I Should Have Done Something" — Carl feels guilty about the death of a hostage who was killed during a robbery.

☐ 24) "Skip to My Lieu" — Lieutenant Murtagh goes on a date with Rachel.

☐ 25) "The Good, the Bad, and the Urkel" — Carl dreams he's in a western shoot-out with Dr. Urkel and Steve.

THIRD SEASON, 1991–92

☐ 1) "Daddy's Little Girl" — Laura gets a crush on Carl's rookie partner.

☐ 2) "Boom" — Carl must deal with a live bomb meant for Murtagh.

☐ 3) "Brain Over Brawn" — Urkel challenges an athlete who likes Laura to a rope-climbing contest.

☐ 4) "Words Hurt" — Urkel sleepwalks and keeps hitting Carl with a rolled-up newspaper.

☐ 5) "The Show Must Go On" — Urkel must fill in for a sick actor, playing Romeo to Laura's Juliet.

☐ 6) "Citizen's Court" — Urkel sues Carl on the TV show "Citizen's Court" after Carl kills his expensive South American bug.

☐ 7) "Choir Trouble" — Rachel is appointed choir director, but her perfectionism drives everyone crazy.

☐ 8) "Old and Alone" — Laura dreams she is 75 years old and alone in the world.

☐ 9) "Making the Team" — Laura joins the cheerleading squad, and Urkel becomes the basketball team's equipment manager.

☐ 10) "Robo-Nerd" — Steve creates a robot version of himself, Urkelbot, that falls for Laura.

☐ 11) "Born to be Mild" — Urkel goes undercover to trap a gang that trashes Rachel's Place.

☐ 12) "The Love God" — Urkel tutors a girl named Vonda so that she'll go out with Eddie.

☐ 13) "A Pair of Ladies" — Urkel plays poker with Carl and his friends.

☐ 14) "Jailhouse Blues" — Eddie and Urkel end up in jail after a joyride with Eddie's cousin Clarence.

☐ 15) "Test of Friendship" — Urkel helps Eddie cheat on a chemistry test.

☐ 16) "My Broken-Hearted Valentine" — Urkel competes with Daniel Wallace to be Laura's Valentine.

☐ 17) "Love and Kisses" — Harriette and Carl finally take the honeymoon they never got to take.

☐ 18) "Brown Bombshell" — Urkel's prison pen pal comes to visit and mistakes Carl for Steve.

☐ 19) "Food, Lies & Videotape" — Carl buys a camcorder, and Urkel takes a home economics class with Laura.

☐ 20) "Woman of the People" — Laura runs for school council president against Cassie Lynn Nubbles.

☐ 21) "The Urkel Who Came to Dinner" — Urkel stays with the Winslows while his family goes on vacation.

Carl, Eddie, and Judy at dinner.

□ 22) "Stop in the Name of Love" — The family must tell Mother Winslow she should no longer drive.

□ 23) "Robo-Nerd 2" — Steve dusts off his Urkelbot and turns him into Urkelcop.

□ 24) "Dudes" — Eddie and Waldo appear on a dating show called "Dudes."

□ 25) "Farewell, My Laura" — Laura and Rachel read Urkel's short story and imagine themselves as characters in a 1940s detective thriller.

12 **How much do you really know about your favorite show?** Take the Official *Family Matters* Trivia Quiz, and find out. Score five points for each correct answer. Then rate yourself on the *Family Matters* scoreboard:

0-20 points: Are you sure you watch *Family Matters?*

21-40 points: OK, so you've seen it once or twice!

41-60 points: You're obviously a loyal *Family Matters* viewer!

61-80 points: Consider yourself a *Family Matters* expert!

81-100 points: Are you sure your name isn't Urkel?

The Official
Family Matters

TRIVIA QUIZ

1) For which 1970s singing group did Telma Hopkins sing backup?

2) What were Kellie Williams' two childhood nicknames?

3) From whom did Jaleel White get Urkel's glasses?

4) In which two movies did Reginald VelJohnson play a police sergeant?

5) What type of music does Darius McCrary's father sing?

6) Carl tries to train Eddie for a career in which sport?
     a) soccer   b) basketball   c) bobsled

7) Laura sets Urkel up with a nerdy girl named
  a) Suzie   b) Myrtle   c) Jolene

8) Urkel sleepwalks and hits Carl with a
  a) pillow   b) pie   c) newspaper

9) Eddie and Waldo appear on a dating show called
  a) Guys   b) Dudes   c) Hunks

10) When Eddie runs for class president, who is his campaign manager?
  a) Laura   b) Urkel   c) Rodney

11) *True or False:* Steve Urkel was named after a real person.

12) *True or False:* Reginald VelJohnson recorded an album of pop songs.

13) *True or False:* Rosetta LeNoire started a children's theater group in New York City.

14) *True or False:* Darius McCrary plays the drums.

15) *True or False:* Kellie Williams has one brother and two sisters.

16) _____ is a police officer whom Carl often works with.

17) Eddie goes to a pool hall with his friend _____.

18) Urkel is made _____ of the school basket-ball team.

19) Eddie's band is called "Eddie and the _____."

20) Laura sells a precious family _____ at a garage sale.

ANSWERS

1) Tony Orlando and Dawn
2) Monkey, Beanie
3) his father
4) *Die Hard I & II*
5) gospel
6) b
7) a
8) c
9) b
10) a

11) true
12) false
13) true
14) true
15) false
16) Lieutenant Murtagh
17) Rodney
18) equipment manager
19) Dreamers
20) quilt

WANT TO WRITE TO *FAMILY MATTERS*?

Write to your favorite *Family Matters* character. You can reach them all at this address:

Family Matters
Studio Fan Mail
1122 South Robertson Blvd.
Suite 15
Los Angeles, CA 90035